BRITISH RAILWAYS STEAMING THROUGH THE SIXTIES

Volume Thirteen

Compiled by

PETER HANDS & COLIN RICHARDS

DEFIANT PUBLICATIONS
190 Yoxall Road,
Shirley, Solihull,
West Midlands

Printed on behalf of Richard Netherwood Ltd by Gorenjski Tisk, Yugolslavia

CURRENT STEAM PHOTOGRAPH ALBUMS AVAILABLE
FROM DEFIANT PUBLICATIONS

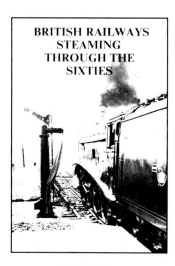

BRITISH RAILWAYS STEAMING THROUGH THE SIXTIES

VOLUME 11
A4 size - Hardback. 100 pages
-180 b/w photographs.
£10.95 + £1.00 postage.
ISBN 0 946857 24 5.

BRITISH RAILWAYS STEAMING THROUGH THE SIXTIES

VOLUME 12
A4 size - Hardback. 100 pages
-182 b/w photographs.
£11.95 + £1.00 postage.
ISBN 0 946857 27 X.

BRITISH RAILWAYS STEAMING THROUGH THE SIXTIES

VOLUME 13
A4 size - Hardback. 100 pages
-182 b/w photographs.
£11.95 + £1.00 postage.
ISBN 0 946857 33 4.

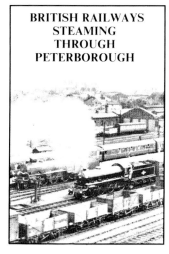

BRITISH RAILWAYS STEAMING THROUGH PETERBOROUGH

A4 size - Hardback. 100 pages
-163 b/w photographs.
£10.95 + £1.00 postage.
ISBN 0 946857 26 1.

BRITISH RAILWAYS STEAMING ON THE WESTERN REGION

VOLUME 3
A4 size - Hardback. 100 pages
-179 b/w photographs.
£10.95 + £1.00 postage.
ISBN 0 946857 25 3.

BRITISH RAILWAYS STEAMING ON THE WESTERN REGION

IN PREPARATION

VOLUME 4

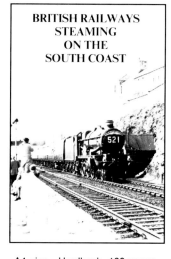

BRITISH RAILWAYS STEAMING ON THE SOUTH COAST

A4 size - Hardback. 100 pages
-182 b/w photographs.
£11.95 + £1.00 postage.
ISBN 0 946857 29 6.

BRITISH RAILWAYS STEAMING ON THE SOUTHERN REGION

IN PREPARATION

VOLUME 3

BRITISH RAILWAYS STEAMING ON THE LONDON MIDLAND REGION

VOLUME 3
A4 size - Hardback. 100 pages
-181 b/w photographs.
£11.95 + £1.00 postage.
ISBN 0 946857 28 8.

BRITISH RAILWAYS STEAMING ON THE LONDON MIDLAND REGION

IN PREPARATION

VOLUME 4

BRITISH RAILWAYS STEAMING ON THE EX-LNER LINES

VOLUME 2
A4 size - Hardback. 100 pages
-187 b/w photographs.
£11.95 + £1.00 postage.
ISBN 0 946857 34 2.

BRITISH RAILWAYS STEAMING ON THE SCOTTISH REGION

IN PREPARATION

VOLUME 1

CURRENT STEAM PHOTOGRAPH ALBUMS AVAILABLE
FROM DEFIANT PUBLICATIONS

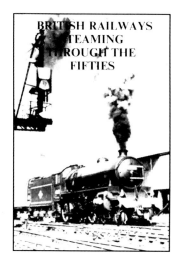

VOLUME 1
A4 size - Hardback. 100 pages
-180 b/w photographs.
£8.95 + £1.00 postage.
ISBN 0 946857 12 1.

VOLUME 2
A4 size - Hardback. 100 pages
-180 b/w photographs.
£8.95 + £1.00 postage.
ISBN 0 946857 13 X.

VOLUME 3
A4 size - Hardback. 100 pages
-180 b/w photographs.
£9.95 + £1.00 postage.
ISBN 0 946857 16 4.

VOLUME 4
A4 size - Hardback. 100 pages
-180 b/w photographs.
£9.95 + £1.00 postage.
ISBN 0 946857 17 2.

VOLUME 5
A4 size - Hardback. 100 pages
-180 b/w photographs.
£9.95 + £1.00 postage.
ISBN 0 946857 22 9.

VOLUME 6
A4 size - Hardback. 100 pages
-180 b/w photographs.
£9.95 + £1.00 postage.
ISBN 0 946857 23 7.

VOLUME 7
A4 size - Hardback. 100 pages
-180 b/w photographs.
£11.95 + £1.00 postage.
ISBN 0 946857 31 8.

VOLUME 8
A4 size - Hardback. 100 pages
-180 b/w photographs.
£11.95 + £1.00 postage.
ISBN 0 946857 32 6.

BRITISH RAILWAYS
STEAMING
THROUGH THE
FIFTIES

IN
PREPARATION

BRITISH RAILWAYS
STEAMING
THROUGH THE
FIFTIES

IN
PREPARATION

BRITISH RAILWAYS
STEAMING
THROUGH CREWE,
DONCASTER,
EASTLEIGH AND
SWINDON

IN
PREPARATION

BRITISH RAILWAYS
STEAMING
FROM ST. PANCRAS
TO ST. ENOCH

IN
PREPARATION

VOLUME 9

VOLUME 10

OTHER TITLES AVAILABLE FROM DEFIANT PUBLICATIONS
PRICES VARY FROM £1 to £3.80 INCLUDING POSTAGE

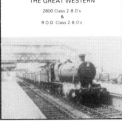

WHAT HAPPENED
TO STEAM

Volume One

THE GREAT WESTERN

2800 Class 2-8-0's
&
R.O.D. Class 2-8-0's

WHAT HAPPENED TO STEAM

This series of booklets, 50 in all, is designed to inform the reader of the allocations, re-allocations and dates of withdrawal of steam locomotives during their last years of service. From 1957 onwards and finally where the locomotives concerned were stored and subsequently scrapped.

BR STEAM SHED ALLOCATIONS

This series lists all individual steam locomotives based at the different parent depots of B.R. from January 1957 until each depot either closed to steam or closed completely. An attractive bookbinder is available for this thirteen book series.

B.R. STEAM SHED
ALLOCATIONS

Part One

WESTERN REGION SHEDS

81A Old Oak Common · 81F Oxford
82A Bristol (Bath Road) · 82F Weymouth
83A Newton Abbot · 83G Penzance

WHAT HAPPENED
TO STEAM

THE
L.N.E.R.
B1 4-6-0's.

WHAT HAPPENED
TO STEAM

THE SOUTHERN
H15, N15, 'KING ARTHURS' S15
& 'LORD NELSON' 4-6-0's.
G16 4-8-0 TANKS.
H16 4-6-2 TANKS.

B. R. STEAM SHED
ALLOCATIONS

Part Four

EASTERN REGION SHEDS

30A Stratford · 30F Parkeston
31A Cambridge · 31E Bury St. Edmunds
32A Norwich · 32G Melton Constable
33A Plaistow · 33C Shoeburyness
34A Kings Cross · 34E Neasden
35A New England · 35C Peterborough (Sptal Bridge)

B. R. STEAM SHED
ALLOCATIONS

Part Five

EASTERN REGION SHEDS

36A Doncaster · 36E Retford
38A Colwick · 38E Woodford Halse
39A Gorton
40A Lincoln · 40F Boston
41A Darnall (Sheffield)

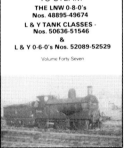

WHAT HAPPENED
TO STEAM

THE LNW 0-8-0's
Nos. 48895-49674
L & Y TANK CLASSES -
Nos. 50636-51546
&
L & Y 0-6-0's Nos. 52089-52529

Volume Forty Seven

WHAT HAPPENED
TO STEAM

THE
LONDON MIDLAND
2F & 3F
0-6-0 TANKS
Nos. 47160-9 & 47200-681

VOLUME FORTY-FIVE

B. R. STEAM SHED
ALLOCATIONS

Part Six

NORTH EASTERN REGION SHEDS

50A York · 50G Whitby
51A Darlington · 51L Thornaby
52A Gateshead · 52F Blyth

B. R. STEAM SHED
ALLOCATIONS

Part Seven

NORTH EASTERN REGION SHEDS

53A Hull (Dairycoates) · 53E Goole
54A Sunderland · 54D Consett
55A Leeds (Holbeck) · 55G Huddersfield
56A Wakefield · 56G Bradford (Hammerton St.)

WHAT HAPPENED
TO STEAM

THE L.N.E.R.
V2 2-6-2's
Nos. 60800-983

VOLUME EIGHT

WHAT HAPPENED
TO STEAM

THE B.R.
CLASS 4 4-6-0's & 2-6-0's
Nos. 75000-79 & 76000-114

B. R. STEAM SHED
ALLOCATIONS

Part Eight

SCOTTISH REGION SHEDS

60A Inverness · 60E Forres
61A Kittybrewster · 61C Keith
62A Thornton Junction · 62C Dunfermline
63A Perth · 63D Oban
64A St. Margarets (Edinburgh) · 64G Hawick
65A Eastfield (Glasgow) · 65J Fort William
66A Polmadie (Glasgow) · 66D Greenock (Ladyburn)
67A Corkerhill (Glasgow) · 67D Ardrossan
68A Carlisle (Kingmoor) · 68E Carlisle (Canal)
St. Rollox Works

B. R. STEAM SHED
ALLOCATIONS

Part Nine

SOUTHERN REGION SHEDS

70A Nine Elms · 70H Ryde (I O W)
71A Eastleigh · 71J Highbridge
72A Exmouth Jct. · 72F Wadebridge
73A Stewarts Lane · 73E Faversham
74A Ashford · 74E St. Leonards
75A Brighton · 75F Tunbridge Wells

WHAT HAPPENED
TO STEAM

Volume Twenty Eight

THE
L.M.S.
8F 2-8-0's
&
Somerset and Dorset
7F 2-8-0's

WHAT HAPPENED
TO STEAM
THE GREAT WESTERN
15xx, 34xx, 84xx, & 94xx
series of
0-6-0 'S
PANNER TANKS
VOLUME THIRTY ONE

B. R. STEAM SHED
ALLOCATIONS

Part Eleven

LONDON MIDLAND REGION
SHEDS

8A Edge Hill (Liverpool) · 8E Brunswick (Liverpool)
9A Longsight (Manchester) · 9G Northwich
10A Springs Branch Wigan · 10D Sutton Oak
11A Carnforth · 11E Lancaster (Green Ayre)
12A Carlisle (Upperby) · 12C Workington

B. R. STEAM SHED
ALLOCATIONS

Part Twelve

LONDON MIDLAND REGION
SHEDS

14A Cricklewood · 14C St. Albans
15A Wellingborough · 15D Bedford
16A Nottingham · 16C Mansfield
17A Derby · 17D Rowsley
18A Toton · 18D Staveley (Barrow Hill)
19A Sheffield (Grimesthorpe) · 19C Canklow

ACKNOWLEDGEMENTS

Grateful thanks are extended to the following contributors of photographs not only for their use in this book but for their kind patience and long term loan of negatives/photographs whilst this book was being compiled.

T. R. AMOS TAMWORTH	B. J. ASHWORTH PENTRYCH	CHRISTOPHER AUDREY *
W. BOYDEN BEXHILL**	B. W. L. BROOKSBANK LONDON	N. L. BROWNE ALDERSHOT
L. BROWNHILL BRIERLEY HILL	KEN ELLIS SWINDON	CHRISTOPHER FIFIELD LONDON
J. M. GASCOYNE HIGH WYCOMBE	A. N. H. GLOVER BIRMINGHAM	J. D. GOMERSALL SHEFFIELD
T. HAILES OULTON BROAD	MIKE HIGSON THE SMOKEBOX	R. W. HINTON GLOUCESTER
H. L. HOLLAND ST. CATHERINES, ONTARIO, CANADA		F. HORNBY NORTH CHEAM
A. C. INGRAM WISBECH	H. N. JAMES IPSWICH	ALAN JONES ***
D. K. JONES MOUNTAIN ASH	R. LEITCH SAWSTON	ERIC LIGHT TICKHILL
A. F. NISBET BRACKLEY	R. PICTON WOLVERHAMPTON	STUART PITCHFORTH SANDAL
W. POTTER BISHOPS CLEEVE	N. E. PREEDY HUCCLECOTE	E. L. RIVETT ARUNDEL
P. A. ROWLINGS ALCONBURY	M. RUTTER BOWER GRANGE	J. SCHATZ LITTLETHORPE
K. L. SEAL ANDOVERSFORD	G. W. SHARPE BARNSLEY	C. P. STACEY STONY STRATFORD
M. S. STOKES MARPLE	A. SWAIN WEMBLEY	D. TITHERIDGE FAREHAM
L. TOLLEY NOT KNOWN	G. H. TRURAN DERBY	S. TURNBULL KIRKINTILLOCH
A. WAKEFIELD DRONFIELD WOODHOUSE	KIT WINDLE LOWER BREDBURY	MIKE WOOD BIRMINGHAM

* Courtesy of the A. C. Ingram collection. ** Courtesy of the Frank Hornby collection.
*** Courtesy of Mike Wood

Front Cover — High summer on the North Wales Main Line. LMS Class 5 4-6-0 No 45247, from 6H Bangor, hugs the coastline at Penmaenmawr with a fitted freight bound for Chester on 20th August 1964. Transferred to 6J Holyhead in April 1965, No 45247 moved to 6A Chester upon the closure of the former shed to steam in December 1966. (T. R. Amos)

ISBN O 946857 33 4

(C) P. B. HANDS/C. RICHARDS 1991
FIRST PUBLISHED 1991

INTRODUCTION

BRITISH RAILWAYS STEAMING THROUGH THE SIXTIES — Volume Thirteen, is the thirteenth in a series of books designed to give the ordinary, everyday steam photographic enthusiast of the 1960's a chance to participate in and give pleasure to others whilst recapturing the twilight days of steam.

In this series, wherever possible, no famous names will be found nor will photographs which have been published before be used. The content and quality of the majority of photographs used will be second to none. The photographs chosen have been carefully selected to give a mixture of action and shed scenes from many parts of British Railways whilst utilising a balanced cross-section of locomotives of GWR, SR, LMS, LNER & BR origins.

As steam declined, especially from 1966 onwards, the choice of locomotive classes and locations also dwindled. Rather than include the nowadays more traditional preserved locomotive photographs in the latter days of steam, the reader will find more locomotives of SR, LMS & BR backgrounds towards the end of the book.

The majority of the photographs used in Volume Thirteen have been contributed by readers of Peter Hands series of booklets entitled "What Happened to Steam" & "BR Steam Shed Allocations" and from readers of the earlier "BR Steaming Through the Sixties" albums. In normal circumstances these may have been hidden from the public eye forever.

The continuation of the 'BR Steaming' series etc., depends upon you the reader. If you feel you have suitable material of BR steam locomotives between 1948-1968 and wish to contribute them towards the series and other future publications please contact either:

Peter Hands,
190 Yoxall Road,
Shirley, Solihull,
West Midlands B90 3RN

OR

Colin Richards
28 Kendrick Close,
Damson Parkway, Solihull,
West Midlands B92 OQD

CONTENTS

NAMEPLATES — Nameplate examples of the five main representatives of British Railways.

1) GWR *Castle* Class 4-6-0 No 5083 *Bath Abbey*. (A. C. Ingram)

2) SR Rebuilt *West Country* Class 4-6-2 No 34004 *Yeovil*. (N.E. Preedy)

3) LMS Unrebuilt *Patriot* Class 4-6-0 No 45504 *Royal Signals*. (A. Wakefield)

4) LNER J36 Class 0-6-0 No 65222 *Somme*. (N.L. Browne)

5) BR *Britannia* Class 4-6-2 No 70037 *Hereward the Wake*. (N. L. Browne)

CHAPTER ONE — 1960

6)   Constructed during grim times of hardship for Great Britain in June 1941, SR Rebuilt *Merchant Navy* Class 4-6-2 No 35002 *Union Castle* (71B Bournemouth) is seen in more peaceful times in 1960 at the head of what is presumably a Bournemouth line express at Waterloo, where the driver is seen attending to some small task on the front end of the locomotive. *Union Castle* had been rebuilt in May 1958 at Eastleigh. (A. C. Ingram)

7) An unusual combination of locomotives for a passenger working on the outskirts of Wednesbury, in the West Midlands, on 1st August 1960. LMS Class 4F 0-6-0 No 44165 (21A Saltley) and LMS Class 4 'Flying Pig' 2-6-0 No 43022 (2B Nuneaton) double-head an excursion past the camera and head towards Dudley (for Dudley Zoo). This special originated from the Nuneaton/Rugby area. (T. R. Amos)

8) Maximum track occupation on a side road by the running shed at 64B Haymarket in October 1960. Centrepiece of the locomotives on view is LNER Gresley inspired A3 Class 4-6-2 No 60057 *Ormonde,* one of the more 'unsung' members of the A3 fleet based at Haymarket. *Ormonde* had acquired a double chimney in October 1958. German smoke deflectors were fitted in September 1961, but withdrawal followed only two years later. (Mike Higson)

9) Safety valves pop and steam sizzles from the front end as SR *Lord Nelson* Class 4-6-0 No 30852 *Sir Walter Raleigh,* from 71A Eastleigh, is made ready for the road by the turntable at 71B Bournemouth on 21st February 1960, with the footplate crew sorting out a problem in the tender. Despite the fine external condition of *Sir Walter Raleigh* condemnation was on the immediate horizon in February 1962. (W. Boyden)

10) Freight power on show in the yard of the former Great Central Railway shed at 41F Mexborough on 16th October 1960. At the forefront are two far from clean WD Class 8F 2-8-0's, one of which can be identified as No 90580. To the left of No 90580 is ex. GC 04/8 Class 2-8-0 No 63612. Both of these Mexborough locomotives were destined to survive in revenue earning service until 1965. The shed died in March 1964. (T. Hailes)

11) The platforms in the right of this picture are all but devoid of human life in the winter of 1960. A young lad and an adult brave the cold conditions at Leeds (Central) on the 16th February to observe the imminent departure of LNER A3 Class 4-6-2 No 60110 *Robert the Devil*, a 34A Kings Cross Pacific, with a London bound express. Pullman stock belonging to the *Yorkshire Pullman,* or *Queen of Scots* is on the left. (Stuart Pitchforth)

12) Sporting the appropriate headboard and route indicator letter and numbers, GWR *Castle* Class 4-6-0 No 5046 *Earl Cawdor,* based at 84A Wolverhampton (Stafford Road), leaves a smokescreen as it departs from Bristol (Temple Meads) between Staple Hill and Mangotsfield with the northbound *Cornishman* on 29th August 1960. Both Staple Hill and Mangotsfield stations were destined for closure in 1966. *Earl Cawdor* demised in 1962. (T. R. Amos)

13) Former Midland Railway freight locomotives on show at the pure Midland setting at 17A Derby (with the unusually shaped roundhouse roof in the background) on 7th August 1960. Nearest the camera is Class 2F 0-6-0 No 58209 (15D Coalville) which has been called in for scrapping. In the left of the frame is Class 3F 0-6-0 No 43373, late of 14E Bedford (condemned in May 1960), which is also awaiting cutting up. (T. R. Amos)

14) Amidst a labyrinth of bridges and electrification gantries BR *Britannia* Class 4-6-2 No 70005 *John Milton* (32A Norwich) lurks on the turntable within the tight confines of Liverpool Street station on Thursday 25th August 1960. To the right of *John Milton* a Brush Type 2 and an LNER N7 Class 0-6-2T can just about be made out. Within a matter of just over two years steam was to be swept away from this major terminus in London. (Christopher Audrey)

15)   For a number of years Brighton shed housed a number of SR Bulleid Light Pacifics for use on the services to and from Plymouth, amongst other express workings. A shroud of white smoke is thrown upwards as Brighton based SR Rebuilt *West Country* Class 4-6-2 No 34008 *Padstow* accelerates a through train for Plymouth out of the station in August 1960. Brighton lost its allocation of these engines by September 1963. (Ken Ellis)

16)   81C Southall is the subject of a shed visit by spotters on 12th September 1960. Apart from the photographer no-one appears to be interested in the presence of 83D Laira (Plymouth) based GWR *Modified Hall* Class 4-6-0 No 7916 *Mobberley Hall*. For spotters living outside the West Country *Mobberley Hall* was a rare beast, being based at Newton Abbot and Laira for many years until sent to 82C Swindon in June 1964. (D. K. Jones)

17) An 'unsung' Drummond Caledonian Railway Class 2F No 57441, from 63A Perth, specially spruced up, is thrust into the limelight at Kirriemuir station (a branch line terminus) at the head of an SLS/RCTS special on 16th June 1960. The leading two carriages are in Caledonian livery. Kirriemuir had closed for normal passenger services during 1952. Kirriemuir Junction station had closed as early as 1864. (F. Hornby)

18) Another elderly locomotive looking in fine fettle, this time in the shape of a SR Wainwright former S.E.C. H Class 0-4-4T, a class that was introduced in 1904. No 31177, from 73J Tonbridge, and equipped with push and pull apparatus, is in charge of an Allhallows to Gravesend Central local passenger train, seen at Sharnal Street on 24th September 1960. No 31177 only survived for a further year or so before being withdrawn. (F. Hornby)

19) The 'bombed' appearance of the shed wall at 52H Tyne Dock looks as if this is all that remains of one of the roundhouses after being 'blitzed' by the Luftwaffe, instead of being part of the normal working environment of the shed on an unknown day in August 1960. 'Sheltering' inside the roundhouse is former North Eastern Railway Q7 Class 0-8-0 No 63470, based at Tyne Dock since a transfer from 52C Blaydon in June 1958. (Ken Ellis)

20) There have been many pictures of GWR *Castle* Class 4-6-0 No 5017 *The Gloucestershire Regiment 28th, 61st* in print, but very few taken at this unusual angle. With a 'driver' and a 'fireman' at the controls, 5017 is photographed from its tender whilst 'dead' on the turntable at Swindon Works in 1960. A longstanding inmate of 85B Gloucester (Horton Road) No 5017 was a victim of the September 1962 purge of withdrawals. (D. K. Jones)

21) Under clear signals, BR Class 5 4-6-0 No 73118 *King Leodegrance,* from 70A Nine Elms, hurries an up fitted van train amidst a plethora of tracks leading past the brick built signalbox at Allbrook Junction in October 1960. The mineral wagon immediately in front of the stairs leading to the signalbox probably supplies coal for keeping the box warm during the colder months. (A. C. Ingram)

22) Fresh from overhaul at Horwich Works and sporting lined livery, LMS Stanier Class 6P5F 2-6-0 No 42975 waits in light steam outside the running shed at 26C Bolton prior to being returned to its home shed at 3D Aston on 5th August 1960. Between September and December of this year No 42975 found no less than three new homes — at 9B Stockport, 5B Crewe (South) and 2A Rugby. It was withdrawn from 9F Heaton Mersey in March 1966. (N. E. Preedy)

23)   Another ex. works locomotive photographed during 1960 is former Robinson inspired Great Central Railway Class 04/8 2-8-0 No 63741, from 36C Frodingham in Lincolnshire. Outshopped from Gorton Works No 63741 is seen with steam to spare travelling through Manchester (Victoria) with a loose-coupled goods, passing a pile of new sleepers. (N. E. Preedy)

24)   With the wind blowing smoke from left to right, this busy scene is captured by the camera in front of the large shed at 73F Ashford on 6th March 1960. Amongst the engines on view, are, from left to right, SR *Schools* Class 4-4-0 No 30925 *Cheltenham* (73B Bricklayers Arms), SR Q1 Class 0-6-0 No 33005 (70C Guildford), BR Class 4 2-6-4T No 80034, SR U1 Class 2-6-0 No 31902 (73J Tonbridge) and LMS Class 2 2-6-2T No 41311. (T. R. Amos)

25)   LMS *Royal Scot* Class 4-6-0 No 45532 *Illustrious,* from 21A Saltley, sets off from Bristol (Temple Meads) with an express bound for Birmingham and Sheffield on a frosty December day in 1961. Made redundant from 1B Camden in November 1959, *Illustrious* was transferred to the Midland lines shed at 16A Nottingham, before moving on to Saltley in June 1961. It ended its working life based at 12B Carlisle (Upperby). (G. W. Sharpe)

26) The grimy external condition of BR Class 3 2-6-0 No 77018, a 67B Hurlford engine, blends in easily with the dull landscape at Bogside racecourse on a murky 26th September 1961. No 77018 is heading the 4.09 pm Kilmarnock to Ardrossan local passenger. A numerical sequence from this class were based at Hurlford for most of their working lives, these being Nos 77015-19. All were withdrawn between March and November 1966. (B. W. L. Brooksbank)

27) Former Southern and London Midland Railway relics are in tandem on a centre road at Exeter (Central) in April 1961. Having observed that the dummy is in the 'off' position the driver of SR Z Class 0-8-0T No 30957 (72A Exmouth Junction) lets steam escape from the cylinders prior to backing off with LMS van No M42488M in the direction of the 1 in 37 incline at the St. Davids end of the station. (D. K. Jones)

28) With the ever present sulphur fumes from exhaust steam escaping from the Gas Works Tunnel in the background, the indicator signal tells us that road M1 is set for LNER A4 Class 4-6-2 No 60029 *Woodcock,* a locally based 34A engine, which is in immaculate condition, prior to setting off from Kings Cross terminus with a down Anglo-Scottish express on 8th April 1961. (D. K. Jones)

29) A close-up picture of LMS *Coronation* Class 4-6-2 No 46238 *City of Carlisle,* an inmate of 12B Carlisle (Upperby), at Crewe in the summer of 1961. *City of Carlisle* is in charge of a Euston to Glasgow (Central) express after a locomotive change at Crewe station. In the background in the maze of tracks between the Chester and West Coast Main Lines is an unidentified LMS Class 5 4-6-0, behind which is the busy, but nowadays preserved signalbox. (Kit Windle)

30)   More Pacific power — this time in the yard at 70A Nine Elms on 25th February 1961. Leading the line is SR Unrebuilt *Battle of Britain* Class 4-6-2 No 34051 *Winston Churchill,* a visitor from 72B Salisbury, on the coal road. Beneath the huge coaling plant is another 'foreigner' SR Rebuilt *Merchant Navy* Class 4-6-2 No 35010 *Blue Star,* from 72A Exmouth Junction. Since being taken out of service both engines have been preserved. (N. L. Browne)

31)   Having only possessed one Pacific — *The Great Bear,* the Great Western was quite happy to 'cock a snoop' at the other major railway companies by being satisfied with their fleet of 4-6-0 passenger engines. *Castle* Class 4-6-0 No 5015 *Kingswear Castle,* an inhabitant of 81A Old Oak Common, poses for the camera in the yard at 89A Shrewsbury in company with locally based GWR 4500 Class 2-6-2T No 5555 on 20th July 1961. (D. K. Jones)

32)   Three months after being equipped with a double chimney at Swindon Works, BR Class 4 4-6-0 No 75006, an 84E Tyseley locomotive (in green livery), finds itself on 'alien' territory at Bevois Valley sidings, Southampton on 18th March 1961, in front of which are the main lines. The Class 4 4-6-0's built by BR were handsome engines which gave more than enough protection for their crews in inclement weather. (T. R. Amos)

33)   Another 'stranger in the camp'. A former Great Central Railway engine 01 Class 2-8-0 No 63867, from 16D Annesley, finds itself on the turntable at 81C Southall on the Western Region on a winter's day in 1961. Presumably No 63867 had found its way to Southall via the G.C. main line, thence via Banbury and the Greenford loop — a rare 'cop' for some spotters. It was withdrawn from Annesley in December 1962. (J. M. Gascoyne)

34) A trio of LMS Class 5 4-6-0's in the shed yard at 63A Perth on 15th April 1961. The only example which can be identified is No 44999, a local engine, in front of which two members of the shed staff pause from their labours to have their photograph taken. Note the tablet catcher affixed to the cab of the engine, used on the single lines to the north of Perth. No 44999 moved on to 67F Stranraer in July 1964. (L. Tolley)

35) GWR *Castle* 4-6-0 No 5077 *Fairey Battle* (87F Llanelly) awaits the 'right away' amongst the semaphores and water columns of the steam age at Swindon station with an up express on Saturday, 30th September 1961. The fireman has taken advantage of the Swindon stop to lay the dust in the tender with hot water from the engine, giving rise to the cloud of steam on top of the tender. (J. D. Gomersall)

36) 'David and Goliath' in company in the shed yard at 71A Eastleigh on 4th March 1961. SR Rebuilt *West Country* Class 4-6-2 No 34021 *Dartmoor,* from 71B Bournemouth, dwarfs GWR 5700 Class 0-6-0PT No 4626, fresh from overhaul at the nearby works and awaiting an opportunity to return to its home shed at 73H Dover. Transferred to the Southern in January 1959, No 4626 ended its days on the same, in March 1964, from Salisbury. (T. R. Amos)

37) Soot, ash and clinker, along with other bric-a-brac, clutter the ash disposal roads in the vast shed yard at 81A Old Oak Common on 27th August 1961, ample evidence of many acts of 'fire cleaning'. Standing over one of the 'goods' roads on this day is an Old Oak based GWR Churchward 4700 Class 2-8-0 No 4704, in company with an unidentified GWR Hawksworth Heavy Shunting 9400 Class 0-6-0PT. (A. Swain)

38) The magnificent arched overall roof at York is the backdrop of this photograph of LNER Peppercorn 1948 built A2 Class 4-6-2 No 60533 *Happy Knight*, equipped with a double chimney and allocated to 36A Doncaster, as it departs in September 1961 with an Edinburgh (Waverley) bound express from Kings Cross. From January 1957 until condemned in June 1963, *Happy Knight* was based at no less than four depots, some more than once. (Kit Windle)

39) To save clogging the main Paddington-Birmingham (Snow Hill) line between Warwick and Hatton with slow moving northbound freights, a relief line was provided for the same during busy periods of main line activity. BR Class 9F 2-10-0 No 92234, a double chimney member of the same, from 84C Banbury, negotiates the relief line with an iron-ore train possibly bound for the furnaces of South Wales during the summer of 1961. (Eric Light)

40)   Fully coaled and serviced for the road, a duet of former Great Northern 02 Class 2-8-0's take a well earned rest out of steam within the cramped confines of the ex. Great Central shed yard at 36E Retford on 27th August 1961. Nearest the camera is locally based No 63949 whilst at the rear is 34F Grantham housed No 63966. For many a year the famous Grantham to High Dyke iron-ore trains were handled by these engines. (T. R. Amos)

41)   LMS *Royal Scot* Class 4-6-0 No 46112 *Sherwood Forester,* from 16A Nottingham, hurries along near Haresfield, between Gloucester and Stonehouse, with the 7.43 am Nottingham (Midland) to Plymouth (North Road) express on 29th July 1961. Ousted from 55A Leeds (Holbeck) by diesels in December 1959, *Sherwood Forester* was ultimately destined to end its working life at 16D Annesley being withdrawn in a sorry state in May 1964. (B. W. L. Brooksbank)

42) A vast stretch of waste ground is seen in the foreground of this photograph taken at Southampton (Central) on 11th March 1961. Judging by the length of the footbridge spanning the station quite a few lines had been removed by this date in time. SR Rebuilt *Merchant Navy* Class 4-6-2 No 35001 *Channel Packet,* from 70A Nine Elms, departs with the down *Bournemouth Belle* from Waterloo. (T. R. Amos)

43) Flanked on either side by locomotives of Great Western origins, WD Class 8F 2-8-0 No 90312 basks in steam in the yard of its home shed at 81E Didcot on 19th March 1961. No 90312 only stayed at Didcot for two months, moving on to 86A Newport (Ebbw Junction), after having arrived from 81C Southall in the March. A further move in October took it to 87F Llanelly. A final movement in June 1962 saw it move to 9G Gorton. (A. N. H. Glover)

CHAPTER THREE — 1962

44)   The driver of LNER Peppercorn A2 Class 4-6-2 No 60526 *Sugar Palm,* a 50A York engine, appears deep in thought as his charge awaits departure from Doncaster with a Kings Cross to Edinburgh (Waverley) express on 13th July 1962. By this date in time many of these expresses were in the hands of diesel power, a fact which helped to hasten the demise of *Sugar Palm* which was withdrawn three months after this picture was taken. (J. Schatz)

45) The powerful and the humble alongside each other next to their home shed at 26B Agecroft on 23rd September 1962. Former L & Y Class 0F 0-4-0ST No 51232, its bufferbeam covered in coal, is overshadowed by LMS *Jubilee* Class 4-6-0 No 45728 *Defiance* (paired with a Fowler tender). For many years a Carlisle based locomotive, *Defiance* had been transferred to Agecroft in July 1962 and like *Sugar Palm* it too was withdrawn in October 1962. (J. Schatz)

46) Early Spring sunshine warms the flat Cheshire countryside to the south of Crewe on the Staffordshire border as BR *Britannia* Class 4-6-2 No 70028 *Royal Star,* newly transferred to 9A Longsight (Manchester) from 21D Aston, darkens the skyline with a lengthy parcels train on the up fast in April 1962. Formerly of 86C Cardiff (Canton), *Royal Star* had been drafted to Aston shed in September 1961. (Kit Windle)

47) GWR *Grange* Class 4-6-0 No 6803 *Bucklebury Grange* in the yard of its home shed at 84E Tyseley on 5th August 1962. Transferred here from 84F Stourbridge in July 1960 *Bucklebury Grange* was destined to remain in the West Midlands for the remainder of its working life. A last transfer in September 1962 took it to 84B Oxley from whence it was taken out of service in September 1965. The end came at the hands of Birds, Long Marston. (R. Picton)

48) A buckled and discarded fire-iron lies unwanted on a concrete base at 36A Doncaster. A tall industrial chimney towers over WD Class 8F 2-8-0 No 90453, from 36C Frodingham. Behind No 90453 is a locally based LNER A1 Class 4-6-2 No 60157 *Great Eastern,* one of the roller bearing equipped members of the class. Although taken by a different photographer to the previous picture, by coincidence the date is the same — 5th August 1962. (J. Schatz)

49) A mixture of electrically controlled colour light signals and manual dummy semaphores, clustered together on a gantry, look down upon SR Rebuilt *West Country* Class 4-6-2 No 34018 *Axminster*, from 70A Nine Elms, on 21st October 1962. *Axminster* is in charge of the 12.35 pm express to Weymouth, seen at the start of its journey at Waterloo. Built in December 1945, *Axminster* was converted to its modified form in September 1958. (J. Schatz)

50) Under the watchful gaze of a seated spotter, LNER A3 Class 4-6-2 No 60059 *Tracery*, a 34A Kings Cross Pacific, coupled to an unidentified locomotive, trundles through York station after leaving York shed in readiness to take up a southbound working on 30th August 1962. Once based on the former Great Central at 38C Leicester G.C., *Tracery* had moved to Kings Cross in April 1957. It is in final form with a double chimney and German smoke deflectors. (J. Schatz)

51) Long before the overhead wires came, LMS *Coronation* Class 4-6-2 No 46221 *Queen Elizabeth,* from 12B Carlisle (Upperby), steams past a signalbox and through Wembley station, eight miles from Euston, with an unidentified express on 5th May 1962. As can be seen, platform three has been extended to accommodate longer trains and it appears to have been done 'on the cheap' utilising wood rather than concrete slabs. (N. L. Browne)

52) A begrimed ex. G.C. workhorse in the shape of 04/1 Class 2-8-0 No 63707 at rest in the yard of its home shed at 40E Colwick on 18th November 1962. In January 1957 No 63707 was allocated to Langwith Junction shed. In May 1960 it went to Immingham before being sent to Colwick from where it was withdrawn in July 1965. No 63707 is from a batch first introduced into service by Robinson in 1911. (J. Schatz)

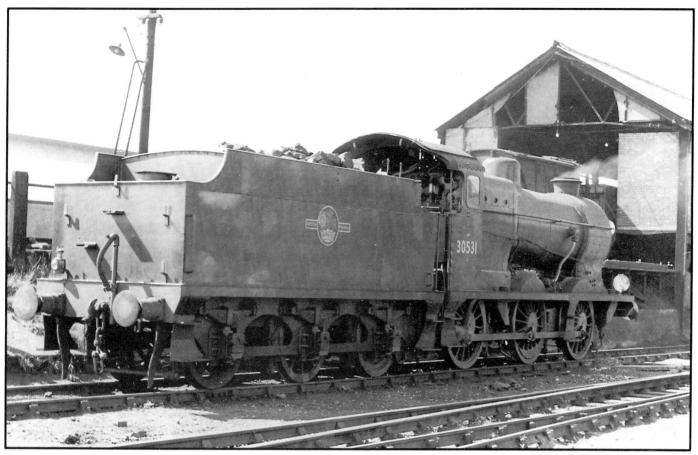

53)   The Maunsell inspired Southern Railway Q Class 0-6-0's were a relatively modern design, being introduced into service in 1938. A smartly turned out locally based example, No 30531, simmers in the yard at 71A Eastleigh on 4th August 1962. Based at Eastleigh for many years without interruption, No 30531 found itself transferred to four different depots between December 1962 and May 1964 being condemned from 75B Redhill in July 1964. (J. Schatz)

54)   Leominster station in June 1962, looking north towards Ludlow, as photographed from Worcester Road bridge. Originally the property of the Shrewsbury & Hereford Railway it was opened in 1853. The lofty white signalbox on one of the platforms can be seen in the distance. Originally, a travelling crane served the track alongside the roadway aside of where GWR 1400 Class 0-4-2T No 1420 (86C Hereford) is shunting. (N. L. Browne)

55) A rarely photographed member of the GWR *Hall* Class 4-6-0's No 4955 *Plaspower Hall,* from 83B Taunton, seen in fine fettle at Exeter St. Davids in July 1962. The driver affixes a local passenger headlamp to the bracket above the smokebox door. *Plaspower Hall* is about to take the through coaches from the down *Cornish Riviera Express* to Newton Abbot, Torquay and Kingswear. (G. H. Truran)

56) The pioneer member of the former North Eastern Railway Q6 Class 0-8-0's No 63340 leaves the outpost of West Auckland with a short freight, the first two items of rolling stock consisting of brakevans, on 27th October 1962. No 63340 is one of sixteen such engines allocated to the local shed, coded 51F. By the time the shed closed on 1st February 1964 their numbers had been reduced to seven. (J. Schatz)

57) The first LMS examples of steam passenger engine power to suffer mass withdrawals as a result of the modernisation programme were the unrebuilt *Patriots*. A number of these engines were dumped at 2A Rugby prior to scrapping Nos 45537/38/41/42/48. Photographed with sacked chimneys on 13th May 1962 are Nos 45537 *Private E. Sykes V.C.* and un-named 45542 which were officially condemned the following month from 2B Nuneaton. (P. A. Rowlings)

58) Steam hisses from the cylinder cocks of BR Class 4 2-6-0 No 76073 which is acting as shed pilot at its home depot at 67E Dumfries on 18th August 1962. The shed had changed codes from 68B exactly two months earlier. No 76073, a longstanding inmate of Dumfries, moved to pastures new at 67C Ayr in April 1966, two months before withdrawal. In common with many Scottish engines the cabside numbers were larger than elsewhere. (J. Schatz)

59)   Two local inhabitants of 75C Norwood Junction await their next rostered workings in front of the running shed on 29th June 1962. In the foreground, with its bunker rather overstocked to say the least, is SR W Class 2-6-4T No 31914 in a very clean external condition. In front of No 31914 is SR U1 Class 2-6-0 No 31900. The latter was withdrawn in 1962. No 31914 moved on to 72A Exmouth Junction in November 1962. (D. K. Jones)

60)   A member of the footplate crew of LMS Rebuilt *Jubilee* Class 4-6-0 No 45735 *Comet,* from 1A Willesden, spares a moment to pose for the camera along with another gent at Crewe on an overcast July day in 1962. The train is the down *Welshman* from Euston to Portmadoc which *Comet* has hauled to Crewe where it is about to retire to Crewe (North) shed being replaced by another locomotive for the remainder of the journey. (Kit Windle)

61)	With their 2-10-0 wheel arrangement the Riddles Ministry of Supply Class 8F heavy freight locomotives looked far more powerful than their 2-8-0 counterparts, but in fact both classes had the same tractive effort of 34,215 lbs. With the fireman dazzled by bright sunshine, one of the 65F Grangemouth examples No 90766 drifts light engine past the camera at Grangemouth on 14th June 1962. (F. Hornby)

62)	Sporting the unusual chalked code of 2J39 on its smokebox GWR 2251 Class 0-6-0 No 2286 is a visitor to 89B Croes Newydd shed in Wrexham on 2nd September 1962. Transferred from 89C Machynlleth to 86C Hereford during this same month No 2286 may well have been in transit to the latter, stopping off at Croes Newydd for servicing. It remained at Hereford until condemned in September 1964. Cashmores, Newport cut it up in early 1965. (J. Schatz)

63)   By the end of 1962 almost a third of the modern GWR *County* Class 4-6-0's had disappeared from their ranks due to withdrawals and the remainder had been eliminated from the depots in Devon and Cornwall. By the last month of 1963 their numbers had been further reduced to less than ten, all based at Swindon. One of the survivors No 1014 *County of Glamorgan* is seen in steam outside Swindon shed, minus front numberplate, on 1st December 1963. (F. Hornby)

64)   A rain drenched scene at Kirkudbright on 13th April 1963 the terminus of the branch from Castle Douglas where LMS Class 4 2-6-4T No 42196 (67E Dumfries) has arrived with the 6.38 am local passenger from Dumfries. With steam condemnations increasing by the month in Scotland No 42196 gained a new lease of life in October 1963 by being drafted to the North Eastern Region where it survived in service until withdrawn in May 1967. (J. Schatz)

65)   Moving from one end of the realm to the other we find ourselves on the Isle of Wight at Ryde. Apart from the running shed there used to be a workshop on the opposite side of the line which served to overhaul the island's locomotives saving the need for them to be transferred to the mainland at Eastleigh for repair. SR 02 Class 0-4-4T No 30 *Shorwell* is almost ready to be returned to traffic on 7th July 1963. (J. Schatz)

66)   Discussion time at 70A Nine Elms on 4th May 1963. The external conditions of the locomotives on view match the mood of the day — grey. Nearest the camera is BR Class 5 4-6-0 No 73087 *Linette* (a name once carried by *King Arthur* Class 4-6-0 No 30752) along with SR Unrebuilt *West Country* Class 4-6-2 No 34007 *Wadebridge*, both inhabitants of Nine Elms shed. (N. L. Browne)

67)   Two GWR 4500 Class 2-6-2T's Nos 5573 and 4569 are lined up in the yard of their home shed at 82D Westbury facing the detached tender from a GWR 4-6-0 on 24th August 1963. Both engines were transferred away before the end of the year, No 4569 to 83E Yeovil (November) and No 5573 to 81C Southall (December). Recoded 83C in October 1963, Westbury shed closed to steam in September 1965. (T. R. Amos)

68) Sunshine and shadow combine in this photograph of SR N Class 2-6-0 No 31819, from 70C Guildford, as it passes through Wimbledon station with an engineers train consisting of empty ballast hoppers after working near Queens Road, Battersea on 11th August 1963. No 31819, rendered redundant from 73H Dover and 75B Redhill during 1961 had moved to Guildford shed from 75A Brighton in January 1962. (A. F. Nisbet)

69) Business services between Dundee and Tayport usually crossed at Newport-on-Tay East. Here, LNER B1 Class No 61340, working tender-first, waits with the 6.40 pm from Tayport as BR Class 4 2-6-4T No 80090 disappears with the 6.00 pm from Dundee Tay Bridge on 28th August 1963. Both of these locomotives are allocated to 62B Dundee Tay Bridge. Note the extended wooden platform, signalbox and rows of gas lamps. (A. F. Nisbet)

70)   The front of the overall glass roof at Carlisle (Citadel) station is all but obscured by the exhaust fumes drifting upwards from the locomotives on view on 20th September 1963. In the left of the picture is LMS Class 5 4-6-0 No 45012, from 12A Carlisle (Kingmoor) on a northbound local passenger train, whilst in the centre, standing light engine, is sister engine No 45210, another Kingmoor inmate. (J. Schatz)

71)   A packed shed yard scene at 72A Exmouth Junction on 10th March 1963 with a selection of rebuilt and unrebuilt Bulleid Pacifics, Tank and other types on show. Centrepiece of the picture is SR Maunsell N Class 2-6-0 No 31875, the last member of the class numerically speaking, an inhabitant of the shed. Condemned from Exmouth Junction in August 1964, No 31875 was despatched to Cashmores, Newport for scrapping later in the year. (J. Schatz)

40

72) A panoramic view of one of the vast shed yards at 36A Doncaster on 8th September 1963. Doncaster owned LNER A1 Class 4-6-2 No 60157 *Great Eastern* heads a line-up of locos which are still active. To the left of *Great Eastern* is a less fortunate Pacific LNER A3 Class 4-6-2 No 60066 *Merry Hampton,* withdrawn this same month and brought to Doncaster from 34F Grantham for cutting up at Doncaster Works. (K. L. Seal)

73) BR Class 5 4-6-0 No 73018, its tender well down in terms of coal supplies, sweeps round a curve beneath the Southern main line at Yeovil Junction and heads for home at Weymouth with a train from Taunton on 17th August 1963. Following a cross country route from Yeovil No 73018 will eventually join the Waterloo to Weymouth main line at Dorchester. It was to serve from just one more depot, at 70C Guildford, prior to withdrawal in July 1967. (B. J. Ashworth)

74)   Weak sunshine reflects off the wet, mirror like platform in the foreground after a heavy shower on 17th August 1963 where a lone traveller observes the passing of SR Rebuilt *Battle of Britain* Class 4-6-2 No 34090 *Sir Eustace Missenden, Southern Railway* (70A Nine Elms) through Clapham Junction at the regulation speed of 40 mph whilst in charge of the 8.22 am express to Bournemouth (West). (A. F. Nisbet)

75)   Complete with headboard mounted above the smokebox GWR *Manor* Class 4-6-0 No 7810 *Draycott Manor,* from 89D Oswestry, threads its way into Shrewsbury station with the Aberystwyth portion of the up *Cambrian Coast Express* on 2nd August 1963. The intricate trackwork, signals, crossing, water column and the small 'dwellings' in the right of the frame help to complete this picture. (K. L. Seal)

76) A row of water columns stand guard in the shed yard at 31B March on 17th August 1963 where a March based LNER Thompson B1 Class 4-6-0 No 61119 is prepared for the road by its footplate crew some three and a half months before the end of steam at the shed. No 61119 had been reallocated to March after the closure of 30A Stratford to steam in September 1962. It died at March shed after closure. (R. Leitch)

77) Looking like a duck out of water amidst the Birmingham Carriage & Wagon built Bo-Bo Class 3 (D6500) diesels, LMS Hughes Class 6P5F 'Crab' 2-6-0 No 42896, from 16A Nottingham, stands on number 5 road outside 73C Hither Green shed in September 1963. Although the shed had lost its own steam allocation two years before this picture was taken, all servicing facilities, including a turntable, were retained for some years. (A. C. Ingram)

78) British Railways built tank engine power occupies all four tracks leading into the shed at 75F Tunbridge Wells on 21st April 1963. Facing the camera are two Class 4 2-6-4 Tanks Nos 80014, resident to Tunbridge, and No 80147 a visitor from 75A Brighton. Upon losing its parent code in September 1963 and becoming a sub-shed of Brighton, No 80014 was transferred under the auspices of the same. (T. R. Amos)

79) Virtually everything which can be seen in this summer 1963 scene at Newton Abbot has been swept away in the passage of time, including the road bridge in the right background. GWR *Hall* Class 4-6-0 No 4930 *Hagley Hall* (82C Swindon) pilots an unidentified D800 *Warship* into the station along with an up express. The major exception to the first statement is of course *Hagley Hall,* since preserved on the Severn Valley Railway. (G. H. Truran)

80) BR *Britannia* Class 4-6-2 No 70039 *Sir Christopher Wren* (40B Immingham) is not too far from its namesake's masterpiece of St. Paul's Cathedral whilst on a visit to London in March 1963. It is seen backing on to the 4.12 pm express to Cleethorpes at platform 8 in Kings Cross station. Awaiting departure from 'The Cross' in an adjacent platform is LNER A3 Class 4-6-2 No 60044 *Melton* (34A Kings Cross) on a Leeds train. (A. F. Nisbet)

81) A general view of the shed yard at 63A Perth on 2nd August 1963, where, judging by the shadows, it is early in the evening during high summer. In the foreground is stored ex. Caledonian Railway Class 3P 4-4-0 No 54466 (condemned in February 1962). Accompanying No 54466 is BR Class 5 4-6-0 No 73007 (a local engine), LNER V2 Class 2-6-2 No 60959, from 61B Aberdeen (Ferryhill), and an unidentified LNER A2 Class 4-6-2. (D. K. Jones).

82) Of the British Railways constructed tank engine classes the Class 2 2-6-2's had the shortest working lives with the class being rendered extinct by December 1965. No 84008, from 15A Leicester (Midland), arrives in the branch platform at Seaton on 18th April 1964 at the head of the 10.15 am local passenger from Stamford Town. No 84008 was taken out of service from Leicester (Midland) in November 1965. (J. Schatz)

83) A sun-soaked scene at 81D Reading on 21st September 1964. In the left of the picture is the running shed where we can catch a glimpse of the resident breakdown crane. The subject matter in the viewfinder is 85A Worcester based GWR *Modified Hall* Class 4-6-0 No 7928 *Wolf Hall* which is making its way to an exit road from the depot. In the right distance is a GWR Tank locomotive. (D. K. Jones)

84) A fine view of most of the immensely long westbound platform at Bournemouth (Central) on 9th July 1964. A trio of locomotives having just left Bournemouth shed and cleared the points have a clear road and cross the pointwork whilst heading west for Branksome sidings. Leading the charge is SR Rebuilt *West Country* Class 4-6-2 No 34032 *Camelford*, from 70E Salisbury, with two BR tender engines in tow. (Alan Jones)

85)   Despite what should have been more than adequate former Caledonian and LMS freight engine power two former North British J37 Class 0-6-0's were allocated to 67C Ayr during the 1960's Nos 64541 (from 65A Eastfield — April 1962) and 64626 (from 65C Parkhead — March 1962). No 64541 was drafted away to 62B Dundee Tay Bridge in June 1963, but No 64626 remained at Ayr until condemned in November 1963. Seen here in store on 17th May 1964. (T. R. Amos)

86)   Displaced Horwich Works shunters LMS Class 2F 0-6-0 Tanks Nos 47164 and 47165 along with Class 2F 0-6-0ST No 11305 await disposal at the rear of 9K Bolton on 8th October 1964, together with LMS Class 3F 0-6-0T No 47549 (rear) and an unidentified Class 4 2-6-4T. Nos 47164/65 were cut up at Cohens, Ickles, Rotherham in January 1965. No 47549 was scrapped at the Central Wagon Co., Ince, Wigan, also in 1965. The fate of No 11305 is unknown. (H. L. Holland)

87)   Another feature of past railway history which has all but disappeared from the scene are the lineside telegraph poles and wires once so common by all railway tracks. A trio of poles lie at different angles on an embankment at Southam, near to Cheltenham, as a filthy GWR 2800 Class 2-8-0 No 3825 (2D Banbury) approaches with a down iron-ore freight on 24th July 1964. (W. Potter)

88)   Sporting its headboard in an unusual location BR *Britannia* Class 4-6-2 No 70020 *Mercury,* from 1A Willesden, darkens the sky as it climbs Stoke bank near to Corby Glen on the East Coast Main Line with the northbound Home Counties Railway Society special to York on 4th October 1964. Corby Glen station, of Great Northern origin and some 100 miles or so from Kings Cross, had closed in 1959. (K. L. Seal)

89)   A mixture of steam and diesel power outside the dilapidated shed structure at 82C Swindon on 26th April 1964. From left to right are an unidentified GWR 2800 Class 2-8-0 along with an unknown English Electric Type 3 D67xx, GWR *County* Class 4-6-0 No 1013 *County of Dorset* and a Beyer Peacock Hymeck Type 3 No D7014. *County of Dorset,* a Swindon engine, is just three months away from withdrawal and oblivion. (J. Schatz)

90)   Grim tenement dwellings along with formidable prison type walls combine to give the onlooker an impression of past poverty at Gateshead on 10th February 1964. No wonder the pop group 'The Animals' made the record 'We've Got To Get Out Of This Place'. A fully serviced LNER V2 Class 2-6-2 No 60940 (52A Gateshead) brightens the scene temporarily as it backs up light engine. It lasted in service until October 1965. (B. J. Ashworth)

91)   Just about the last Southern Region cross country route to remain in steam hands was the line from Redhill to Reading in
       terms of passenger services and the trains were hauled by a variety of locomotives from SR, GWR and BR Classes. A female
       passenger appears to be deep in thought as she walks towards SR N Class 2-6-0 No 31411 (75B Redhill) at North Camp
       (Farnborough) in September 1964. (A. F. Nisbet)

92)   A small section of one of the two huge roundhouses at 50A York is captured on film on 19th May 1964 where we see one
       of York's allocation of BR Class 9F 2-10-0's at rest. Adjacent to No 92206 (fitted with a double chimney) is a visiting LNER
       B1 Class 4-6-0 No 61215 *William Henton Carver* (stripped of nameplates), from 56B Ardsley, a depot it was to survive at until
       rendered surplus to requirements in March 1965. (H. L. Holland)

93)   A combination of Hawksworth and Stanier designed power are gathered together at Chester station on an unspecified day in June 1964. GWR *Modified Hall* Class 4-6-0 No 7914 *Lleweni Hall* (82E Bristol Barrow Road) faces LMS Class 8F 2-8-0 No 48474 (2A Tyseley) and LMS *Royal Scot* Class 4-6-0 No 46152 *The King's Dragoon Guardsman* (6J Holyhead). The LMS engines appear to be hissing in protest at the GWR usurper. (Kit Windle)

94)   Despite the ever growing legions of main line diesel power Newcastle-upon-Tyne still hosted Pacific powered passenger engines from Gateshead shed, albeit in a much reduced role during 1964. With the impressive New Castle in the distance, LNER A3 Class 4-6-2 No 60085 *Manna,* in dreadful external condition, awaits departure amidst colour light signalling with a 'stopper' bound for Berwick-on-Tweed. (B. J. Ashworth)

95) The railways over the years have been accused time after time of not being prepared for the hazards brought by sudden falls of snow, but the authorities at Eastleigh Works could not be accused of dragging their heels as can be seen by this shot of SR Q Class 0-6-0 No 30548 (70D Eastleigh) fitted with a large snowplough. However, the date is 12th September 1964 and how much snow was expected in the near future is anybody's guess! (W. Boyden)

96) A fine close-up shot of LMS Hughes Class 6P5F 'Crab' 2-6-0 No 42795 at home alongside its shed at 67B Hurlford (Kilmarnock) on 17th May 1964. In January 1957 this locomotive was the property of the North Eastern Region at 55A Leeds (Holbeck). After moves to 55C Farnley Junction in June 1959, 55E Normanton in March 1962 and 55D Royston three months later, No 42795 was required by the Scottish Region transferring to 67B in November 1963. (W. Boyden)

97)	Desecration of a once magnificent locomotive at 70D Eastleigh on 12th September 1964 where a withdrawn SR Unrebuilt *Battle of Britain* Class 4-6-2 No 34061 *73 Squadron,* late of Eastleigh shed, is espied by the photographer having had its nameplates removed and 'Battle of Britain' crest cut out by the use of a blowtorch. After a period of storage at Eastleigh No 34061 was moved to Woods, Queenborough, Kent for scrapping. (W. Boyden)

98)	Two passenger trains appear to be on a collision course at Gloucester (Central) station on 27th June 1964. However, this is normal operating practice not a signalman's blunder with the two trains being protected by the elevated signals on the canopy. GWR 5100 Class 2-6-2T No 4157, from 86G Pontypool Road, arrives with a local from Hereford with GWR 5700 Class 0-6-0PT No 3693 (85B Gloucester-Horton Road) on a Cheltenham working. (W. Potter)

99)   An unkempt looking 16B Annesley based BR Class 9F 2-10-0 No 92067 has steam to spare as it rattles a Class 8 loose-coupled mineral train past Wilford signalbox, just south of Nottingham (Victoria) on the former Great Central main line heading southbound on 21st July 1964. By this stage in time the writing was on the wall for this famous route with all but total closure on the horizon — no wonder the engine is unkempt. (K. L. Seal)

100)   The condition of the roof atop the roundhouse structure at 51C West Hartlepool leaves something to be desired on 6th September 1964. One of West Hartlepool's fleet of ex. North Eastern Railway Q6 Class 0-8-0's No 63391 simmers in front of an entrance to the roundhouse. Access to the depot, with its yard, roundhouse and straight running shed is via Mainsforth Terrace which runs alongside the same to the right of this picture. (T. R. Amos)

CHAPTER SIX — 1965.

101)   With the fireman nowhere to be seen the driver of SR Rebuilt *West Country* Class 4-6-2 No 34034 *Honiton,* a 70D Eastleigh
        engine, keeps an eye open on the water column hose and a hand on the control wheel in readiness to turn off the supply as
        soon as the tender is filled. *Honiton* is in charge of a Waterloo to Salisbury express at Basingstoke on Whit Monday, 7th June
        1965. (J. D. Gomersall)

102) Its life's work over former Robinson Great Central Class O4/8 2-8-0 No 63691 lies discarded on a back road at its home shed of 41J Langwith Junction on 4th August 1965. Allocated to the depot from 40D Tuxford in January 1959 No 63691 had been condemned in June 1965. Stored at Langwith for some six months it was removed and taken to Wards, Killamarsh for disposal being destroyed by the same in January 1966. (Ken Ellis)

103) On the evening of Sunday 13th July 1965, one of the surviving members of the LMS *Jubilee* Class 4-6-0's No 45694 *Bellerophon*, from 56A Wakefield, approaches Cherry Tree Junction, to the west of Blackburn, with an excursion returning from Blackpool to Wakefield. On the left, the former Lancashire and Yorkshire Union Railway line from Wigan curves in to meet the Lancashire and Yorkshire Line. (H. L. Holland)

104)	The fast approaching end of steam in South Wales is magnificently captured in this panoramic portrait taken at Swansea (High Street) around September/October 1965. A spruced up GWR *Grange* Class 4-6-0 No 6859 *Yiewsley Grange* (86E Severn Tunnel Junction), minus nameplates, runs into the station with an RCTS special. This may well have been the last steam working into Swansea! Loco withdrawn in November 1965. (G. H. Truran)

105)	Yet another locomotive stripped of nameplates is BR *Britannia* Class 4-6-2 No 70053 *Moray Firth,* from 2D Banbury, seen passing Swan Village in the West Midlands with a West of England to Wolverhampton (Low Level) holiday train on 21st August 1965. This was the last summer of through steam hauled passenger trains on former Great Western routes like the North Warwick line to the West Midlands. (T. R. Amos)

106) There is enough daylight filtering through the roof of the large running shed at 70A Nine Elms on 7th March 1965 to photograph SR Q Class 0-6-0 No 30530 without the aid of a flash on the camera. For No 30530, allocated to Nine Elms from 70F Bournemouth in January 1964, it is the end of the road having been taken out of service some three months before this picture was taken. (C. P. Stacey)

107) One of the last surviving LMS Fowler Class 4 2-6-4 Tanks still in service, No 42406, is noted outside its home at 56A Wakefield on 9th May 1965 in company with an unidentified, due to having no nameplate, LMS *Jubilee* Class 4-6-0. By 1965 the rush was on to 'spot' and record on film as many steam locomotives as possible for they were being withdrawn by the score as each week passed by. No 42406 demised in September 1965. (T. R. Amos)

108) There were many steam sheds in and around the city of Sheffield before the diesels arrived on the scene and eliminated them. One such depot is 41D Canklow, once the property of the Midland Railway. Seen in steam in the yard on 25th July 1965 is LNER B1 Class 4-6-0 No 61051, a visitor to the shed from 41J Langwith Junction. After being withdrawn in February 1966 No 61051 became Departmental loco No 31. (E. L. Rivett)

109) With the bleak moorland partially shrouded in mist the since preserved LMS *Royal Scot* Class 4-6-0 No 46115 *Scots Guardsman*, of 12A Carlisle (Kingmoor), adds its own contribution to the atmosphere with a twin cloud of smoke emerging from its double blastpipe on an unknown day in 1965. *Scots Guardsman* appears to be struggling for adhesion at the head of a fitted freight at Horton-in-Ribblesdale. (D. K. Jones)

110) Despite being closed as early as 1930, the overgrown platforms at Castle Donington and Shardlow station in the East Midlands are still partially intact thus enabling the photographer to take advantage of the same to record this picture of BR Class 9F 2-10-0 No 92122, from far away 8H Birkenhead, as it hurries through with a Class 8 mineral hopper freight on 16th October 1965. (T. R. Amos)

111) Towards the end of steam on BR many aspects of work associated with the same were rather neglected such as in this shot taken of the turntable at 6D Shrewsbury shed in the summer of 1965. The tracks within the vicinity of the same are well taken over by weeds, something which would never have happened in prouder bygone times. On the turntable is an 81F Oxford GWR *Hall* Class 4-6-0 No 6923 *Croxteth Hall*. (G. W. Sharpe)

112)   A 10H Lower Darwen stalwart BR Class 4 2-6-0 No 76084 leaks steam in a cold yard at its home shed on 2nd March 1965 where there is a sprinkling of late winter snow on the ground. Nos 76080-84 spent most of their active working lives from this shed. No 76084 parted company with Lower Darwen during this same month, being drafted to less likeable surroundings at 8G Sutton Oak. (H. L. Holland)

113)   At its height 12B Carlisle (Upperby) was a hub of activity with steam locomotives galore arriving for servicing and departing for this, that and the other working, but by 25th April 1965 it was a shadow of its former self. LMS Class 2 2-6-2T No 41264, allocated to Upperby from 8M Southport two months earlier, is employed in the mundane task of shunting empty coal wagons under the watchful eyes of a shunter at the shed. (T. R. Amos)

114) With steam all but eliminated from the Welsh Valleys, one of the survivors, GWR 1600 Class 0-6-0PT No 1669 (87F Llanelly) is a matter of days away from withdrawal as it is employed on a Stephenson Locomotive Society special (wagons and brakevans) at Cwmmawr on 25th September 1965. This station of Burry Port and Gwendraeth Valley origin had closed in 1953 with nature soon taking over as can be seen clearly. (J. Schatz)

115) LNER V2 Class 2-6-2 No 60876, one of many such locomotives once based at 50A York, nears Thrybergh Junction on the ex. Great Central Doncaster to Sheffield line with the 18.50 hours York to Swindon mail train in August 1965, the last regular steam rostered passenger train on the route — dieselised the same month. No 60876 was condemned two months later and scrapped at Cashmores, Great Bridge in January 1966. (M. S. Stokes)

116) A begrimed WD Class 8F 2-8-0 No 90396, one of the fleet of the same allocated to 56A Wakefield, wheels a loose-coupled Class 8 mineral train along at Copley on 18th August 1965. Copley, a former Lancashire & Yorkshire product on the line between Halifax and Luddendenfoot in the Calder Valley, had lost its station facilities as far back as 1931. No 90396 was destined to soldier on at Wakefield until June 1967. (R. W. Hinton)

117) 81C Southall based GWR *Modified Hall* Class 4-6-0 No 7922 *Salford Hall,* bereft of name and shedplates, having just been serviced, is ready for its next rostered duty in the shed yard at 2B Oxley in July 1965. Having been based at Southall shed since December 1962, *Salford Hall* made a final move to 81F Oxford in August 1965 being taken out of service from there at the end of the year. (L. Brownhill)

118) On shed at 70F Bournemouth on 2nd March 1965 at rest in the yard as taken from the long platform opposite the depot is SR Bulleid Rebuilt *Merchant Navy* Class 4-6-2 No 35026 *Lamport & Holt Line,* a locomotive resident to 70G Weymouth, in a rather more than scruffy external condition. Behind *Lamport & Holt Line,* is one of Bournemouth's allocation of LMS Ivatt Class 2 2-6-2 Tanks. (D. K. Jones)

119) LNER A4 Class 4-6-2 No 60007 *Sir Nigel Gresley,* from 61B Aberdeen (Ferryhill), leaves Kinnaber Junction, on the Glasgow (Buchanan Street)-Aberdeen main line, with the up *Bon Accord* express on 10th June 1965. Waiting at signals at the junction with a freight from the Montrose direction is LNER B1 Class 4-6-0 No 61172, from 62B Dundee Tay Bridge. *Sir Nigel* is of course still with us, but No 61172 demised in December 1965. (K. L. Seal)

120) The large depot at 50A York was destined to continue with steam on its books until the beginning of July 1967, but as the weeks and months progressed there were less and less demands for the services of steam from the shed. This 1966 picture of the inside of the roundhouse shows how little steam was left with rows of empty tracks to the left of the frame. On show is York based LNER V2 Class 2-6-2 No 60831. (Stuart Pitchforth)

121) A modern office block and other dwellings look down upon the railway scene at Southampton on 13th August 1966. A filthy SR Rebuilt *Merchant Navy* Class 4-6-2 No 35013 *Blue Funnel,* a 70F Bournemouth locomotive, emerges from Southampton Tunnel with the down *Bournemouth Belle* Pullman train and threads its way over the soon to be energised third rails, a power source which was to mean the end for *Blue Funnel* and her sisters. (B. J. Ashworth)

122) The Ivatt Class 4 'Flying Pig' 2-6-0's served from depots on all regions with the exception of the Southern and Western and withdrawals did not reduce any of their numbers until quite late in the day, in 1963. No 43141, once based in Scotland, had, by October 1963, found its way to the North Eastern Region. On 20th September 1966 it is seen in the yard of its home shed at 55E Normanton. (A. Wakefield)

123) A line-up of grimy BR Standard locomotives alongside the running shed at 67A Corkerhill on 15th July 1966 are partially hidden by stacks of BR stores. Facing the camera is the pioneer Class 4 2-6-4T No 80000, with a more than unusual style of front numberplate. Behind No 80000, a Corkerhill engine, is a fellow inmate from the same class, No 80063. (C. P. Stacey)

124) The houses on the hill in the background have a fine view of the shed and yard at 9L Buxton. On show in the yard on 10th April 1966 is a resident LMS Class 8F 2-8-0 No 48744 which had been drafted to the shed from 9D Newton Heath in January of the same year. It ended its days at 9K Bolton after being transferred there in March 1968, being withdrawn immediately upon arrival — a paper transfer perhaps! (C. P. Stacey)

125) The three immaculate white discs attached to the front of SR Rebuilt *West Country* Class 4-6-2 No 34098 *Templecombe,* from 70D Eastleigh, only help to enhance the bedraggled and sorry state of the engine as it passes a railway worker whilst approaching Bournemouth (Central) station with a parcels train on 16th August 1966. Constructed in December 1949 and rebuilt in June 1961, *Templecombe* was withdrawn in June 1967. (T. R. Amos)

126) Bright summer sunshine envelopes the countryside near to Farnley Junction as a 56D Mirfield based LMS Class 5 4-6-0 No 44946 storms past the camera with an empty coaching stock special bound for Bury on 9th July 1966. The line in the background is the Leeds to Doncaster route. Two months later No 44946 found itself at a new home — at 56F Low Moor. It was withdrawn from 56A Wakefield in June 1967. (M. S. Stokes)

127) On the Isle of Wight there are several towns which are not all that they seem to be: There is 'Newport' you cannot bottle, 'Cowes' you cannot milk and 'Freshwater' you cannot drink! There is also a steam locomotive named after the latter and this CAN drink fresh water. SR 02 Class 0-4-4T No 35 *Freshwater* is prepared for the road in the ash-strewn yard at 70H Ryde on 21st August 1966. (B. J. Ashworth)

128) With steam leaking from various points, former North Eastern Railway J27 Class 0-6-0 No 65812 (52F Blyth) waits at an unusual signal gantry at North Blyth whilst travelling light engine on 4th August 1966. In the background is North Blyth shed with a sister locomotive apparently hemmed in between some coal wagons. A once longstanding inmate of 52E Percy Main No 65812 had been transferred to Blyth in February 1965. (N. E. Preedy)

129) It is not often that a BR Class 9F 2-10-0 was noted travelling tender-first on a freight train, but this is the case with No 92247, fitted with a double chimney, as it approaches Banbury station on 29th April 1966. Constructed in December 1958 it remained at Western Region orientated sheds like Banbury until September 1966 when it was drafted to 9D Newton Heath. The LMR authorities were not impressed and it was soon withdrawn. (D. K. Jones)

130) Amongst the various representatives of loco classes used from time to time as works shunters at Crewe were examples from the LMS Class 4F 0-6-0's. No 44525, complete with the yellow stripe on its cab which prohibited its use south of Crewe, is seen in a part of the massive complex on 20th September 1966, one month before it was taken out of service. Scrapping came at the hands of Drapers, Hull in March 1967. (D. K. Jones)

131) SR Rebuilt *Merchant Navy* Class 4-6-2 No 35030 *Elder Dempster Lines* (70G Weymouth) pulls out of Waterloo with the 12.30 pm *Bournemouth Belle* on Monday, 29th August 1966. The panoramic view of the mighty terminus is taken from the eighth floor of 'Canterbury House' flats which overlook the station, a most desirable railway observation residence, which is more than can be said of some of the other properties in front of it. (J. D. Gomersall)

132) Engine and brakevan pass the camera at Freemans Crossing, Blyth on 8th October 1966. In charge of the brakevan is LNER B1 Class 4-6-0 No 61014 *Oribi,* minus plates, from 52F Blyth a depot it had been based at since a transfer from 56F Low Moor in August 1966. Freemans Crossing is situated in a conglomeration of freight only lines leading to North Blyth, Cambois Power Station and Winning. (M. Rutter)

133) With the external condition of the locomotive speaking for itself BR Class 5 4-6-0 No 73092, a visitor to 70D Eastleigh from 70C Guildford, sports immaculate white discs on its bufferbeam whilst awaiting its next call to duty on 25th May 1966. From January 1957 until October 1965, when No 73092 had been allocated to Guildford, it had worked from Patricroft, Shrewsbury, Gloucester, Bath and Eastleigh sheds. (D. Titheridge)

134) Despite being officially closed to steam on 3rd January 1966 the shed at 85B Gloucester (Horton Road) still retained servicing facilities for the odd steam visitor. Seen in steam by the turntable in the yard on 13th February 1966 is LMS Class 8F 2-8-0 No 48673, from 16E Kirkby. For steam starved fans on the Western Region this must have been a splendid sight even if the locomotive was 'inferior' in quality to the Swindon products. (R. Picton)

135)   A shroud of choking sulphurous fumes seep out of the mouth of Wednesbury Tunnel after BR Class 4 2-6-0 No 76037, a
        2B Oxley (Wolverhampton) engine, emerges in full cry at the head of a mixed freight and heads for Swan Village on the
        Birmingham (Snow Hill) to Wolverhampton (Low Level) main line on 31st May 1966. Shortly before the closure of Oxley
        No 76037 moved on to 6A Chester and thence to 6C Croes Newydd. (T. R. Amos)

136)   Steam power was very much on the retreat in Scotland when this picture was taken by the massive coaling plant at 65A Eastfield
        (Glasgow) where we see a line-up of stored and condemned locomotives. Leading the redundant quartet on show is former
        North British Railway J38 Class 0-6-0 No 65905 on 12th August 1966. It is probably in transit from 62A Thornton Junction
        to Shipbreaking Industries, Faslane for cutting up (E. Rivett)

137)   9F Heaton Mersey shed on the morning of 8th October 1966 with a variety of LMS Class 5 and Class 8F locomotives in steam in front of the running shed. Heaton Mersey based LMS Class 5 4-6-0 No 45114 is in company with LMS Class 4 'Flying Pig' 2-6-0 No 43112, from 5D Stoke. The structure in the foreground by the abandoned water column is possibly a primitive type of loading gauge. (M. S. Stokes)

138)   A fully lined out and clean SR USA Class 0-6-0T No 30073, a resident of the near at hand shed at 70D Eastleigh, is employed on a trip freight working at Eastleigh on 17th August 1966. Once of 71I Southampton Docks, No 30073 had transferred to Eastleigh in June 1963 along with the majority of the class, including the Departmental ones. Despite its smart external appearance it was taken out of traffic in December 1966. (D. Titheridge)

CHAPTER EIGHT — 1967

139) A crude pathway leads directly into the shed at 9E Trafford Park in Manchester on 26th June 1967 where the first two locomotives on view are from the ranks of the condemned. Rendered surplus to traffic requirements both LMS Class 4 2-6-4 Tanks Nos 42644 and 42656 had been withdrawn from service during March and May 1967 respectively. Both of these locomotives were scrapped at the hands of Cashmores, Great Bridge. (M. S. Stokes)

140) Observing the 20 mph speed limit ex. North Eastern Railway J27 Class 0-6-0 No 65879 negotiates the points with caution at Ryhope Grange Junction, Sunderland with a trip hopper working towards the end of steam in the north east — taken on 1st September 1967. Condemned from Sunderland shed during the same month No 65879 was transported to Stockton-on-Tees for scrapping by the firm of Thompsons in November 1967. (T. R. Amos)

141) Amidst all the doom and gloom of the death throes of steam in Britain we find a glimmer of hope for the future in the shape of the newly overhauled and preserved former Lancashire & Yorkshire Class OF 0-4-0ST No 51218, withdrawn from 87A Neath in September 1964 and destined for the Keighley & Worth Valley Railway. Its condition is in stark contrast to the LMS Class 8F 2-8-0 and LMS Class 5 4-6-0 No 45425, seen at 9D Newton Heath on 20th February 1967. (N. E. Preedy)

142) Quadruped tracks in a cutting at Shipley, between Leeds and Skipton on 3rd May 1967. One of the tracks is temporarily occupied by BR Class 9F 2-10-0 No 92118, a resident of 10A Carnforth, at the head of a fitted freight. Originally allocated to depots on the Midland Division, No 92118 moved to the Birmingham area in January 1962. From there it moved north to Carnforth, its final home, in November 1966. (N. E. Preedy)

143) Steam escapes from the cylinder cocks as SR Rebuilt *Merchant Navy* Class 4-6-2 No 35014 *Nederland Line,* from 70G Weymouth, prepares to move its load, the 10.30 am two hour express to Bournemouth out of Waterloo on 12th March 1967, a sight which was all too soon to disappear for ever from this last bastion of London terminus steam. Built in February 1956, *Nederland Line* was rebuilt at Eastleigh in July 1956. (J. M. Gascoyne)

144) Its life's work all but at an end, former North Eastern Railway Q6 Class 0-8-0 No 63455 sports two brand new lamps on its bufferbeam inside the 'bombed' out roundhouse at its home shed 52H Tyne Dock on 11th June 1967. A once longstanding regular at Consett shed, No 63455 had been reallocated to Tyne Dock upon the closure of the former in May 1965. It was condemned from Tyne Dock in July 1967. (N. E. Preedy)

145) How the mighty are fallen — 64A St. Margarets (Edinburgh) on 11th July 1967 a few weeks after official closure. Only two steam locomotives are still to be seen on the depot, ex. NBR J36 Class 0-6-0 No 65234 (ex. 64F Bathgate) and LMS Class 5 4-6-0 No 44997, late of 63A Perth, both employed as stationary boilers. The latter is photographed in the shed yard from an unusual angle facing the derelict antiquated coaler. (S. Turnbull)

146) During the late fifties and up to withdrawal in September 1967 LMS Class 8F 2-8-0 48531 served at 8B Warrington, 8C Speke Junction, 1A Willesden, 2C Stourbridge, 2B Oxley and 5B Crewe (South) being photographed at the latter location in August 1967. Two months after being condemned it was despatched to Cashmores, Great Bridge, like many others before, for scrapping. Today there are few signs that the shed ever existed. (J. M. Gascoyne)

147) By the end of 1966 the LMS Class 4 2-6-4 Tanks were almost extinct as a breed and by October 1967 they were all gone with the exception of Nos 42073, 42085 and 42500 which are preserved. On 29th April 1967, two of them are employed in tandem on an RCTS special, Nos 42616 and 42647, both 8H Birkenhead engines, seen here leaving Wrexham travelling northbound. No 42647 was withdrawn the following month but No 42616 lived for a while longer at 56F Low Moor. (T. R. Amos)

148) In BR days the Southern employed engines from GWR, LMS and BR origins to supplement its own home bred types. One such 'foreign' example is LMS Ivatt Class 2 2-6-2T No 41284, from 70A Nine Elms, being employed as a station pilot at Waterloo on 14th January 1967. From January 1957 No 41284 had found work from 27A Bank Hall, 24G Skipton and 14D Neasden sheds, before arriving on the Southern in June 1961. (Mike Wood)

149) The skyline around Birkenhead shed was always dominated by a number of large gas holders, seen here in the right of the picture. In the background is the former Great Western section of this large running shed. Taking refreshment in the yard is former Crosti-boilered BR Class 9F 2-10-0 No 92022, minus numberplate. Simmering next to No 92022 is a conventional 9F No 92056 (12A Carlisle-Kingmoor) — The date is 6th May 1967. (N. E. Preedy)

150) Once a proud member of the fleet of *Britannia's* based at 86C Cardiff (Canton) on the Western Region No 70027 *Rising Star*, from 12A Carlisle (Kingmoor), is noted in steam, stripped of nameplates, in the yard at 5B Crewe (South) on 2nd June 1967 with its protective canvas sheet draped round the tender. Behind *Rising Star* is LMS Class 8F 2-8-0 No 48018, a locomotive allocated to Crewe (South). (N. E. Preedy)

151) It is hard to believe but precisely one week before this picture was taken on 8th July 1967 LMS Class 5 4-6-0 No 44679 was noted in steam at 8F Springs Branch Wigan and here it is dumped on a back road stripped of motion, shed and numberplate in a shocking condition. Despite the state of the locomotive it wasn't officially condemned until September 1967. It was cut up at Cashmores, Newport in June 1968. (Christopher Fifield)

152) An interesting shot of a 'bulled up' ex. NBR J36 Class 0-6-0 No 65345, withdrawn from 62A Thornton Junction in June 1967, at work in October 1967 some months after steam had finished in Scotland. No 65345 is seen at Uplawmoor on the old Caledonian line from Glasgow (St. Enoch) to Ardrossan with two restored coaches being filmed by the BBC for a future episode of 'Dr. Finlay's Casebook'. It was cut up the next month. (N. E. Preedy)

153) A busy scene at Woking station on 3rd June 1967 where photographers and spotters alike gather to record the dying days of steam on the Southern Region. Smoke pours from the large diameter funnel of name and numberless SR Bulleid Rebuilt *Battle of Britain* Class 4-6-2 No 34089 *602 Squadron*, in a very presentable condition from 70E Salisbury as it heads westbound with a down express as its driver ponders his future. (B. J. Ashworth)

154) Despite the mass withdrawals of the sixties even at this late stage in time 9H Patricroft shed still had a considerable number of the robust BR Class 5 4-6-0's on its books, mostly of the Caprotti variety. One of the latter, No 73131 storms towards the camera at Mirfield on 18th October 1967 with a lengthy fitted freight. The engine still has its numberplate affixed though the shedplate has been removed. (N. E. Preedy)

155) Locally based LMS Class 4 'Flying Pig' 2-6-0 No 43125 stands in light steam in the yard at 55E Normanton on 2nd June 1967, three months prior to withdrawal. Although the water column is still in use the brazier next to it will never again be used for the purpose it was designed for, for by the time freezing conditions next arrived the shed will have died. The running shed in the background is rather run down judging by the state of the roof. (A. Wakefield)

156) The end of the road for two LNER B1 Class 4-6-0's Nos 61014 *Oribi* and 61386 after withdrawal from service at 52F North Blyth in December 1966. They are dumped unwanted in the shed yard on 11th March 1967 prior to being despatched for scrapping. Although sharing the same fate they were sent to different yards, No 61014 to Drapers, Hull and No 61386 to Willoughbys, Choppington (Guide Post). (M. Rutter)

157) A gaggle of enthusiasts observe the comings and goings of a Southern Region light Pacific at Basingstoke on 13th May 1967. An advertising hoarding looks down upon the deserted shed yard as Unrebuilt *West Country* Class 4-6-2 No 34102 *Lapford,* from 70D Eastleigh, devoid of nameplates from its air-smoothed casing, drifts by the camera. Condemned in July *Lapford* was stored at 70E Salisbury until March 1968 before being despatched to Buttigiegs, Newport for disposal. (D. Titheridge)

158) Pure nostalgia at 8A Edge Hill (Liverpool) on 20th April 1968, a few short days before the shed bade farewell to steam power. One wonders what happened to these three railwaymen when steam finished, and what they are doing today? The trio are 'posing' for the camera on the footplate of a visiting LMS Class 8F 2-8-0 No 48720, from 9F Heaton Mersey, beneath the coaling plant at Edge Hill. (J. M. Gascoyne)

159) The two tracks in the centre of this picture consist of a more modern type with up to date clips holding the rails to the sleepers, whilst to the left and right of the same the other tracks are secured by the older 'bullhead' joints, rarely seen today. LMS Class 8F 2-8-0 No 48773, a local engine, passes Bolton shed (out of sight to the left) with a lengthy rake of fitted freight wagons in the Spring of 1968. (Christopher Fifield)

160) Moving a matter of yards from the previous picture the camera lens is pointed towards the entrance to the depot at Bolton, coded 9K at this stage in time. Two LMS types flank one of the inhabitants of the shed LMS Class 8F 2-8-0 No 48652, one of the few examples which were fitted with a permanent small snowplough — never to be used in anger again. This engine died at Bolton in June 1968. (Christopher Fifield)

161)	Despite the extensive use of wood in the construction of steam motive power depots it is somewhat surprising that there were so few fires involving them, Preston shed being one of the few to be badly damaged. The interior of 9H Patricroft is a prime example of a fire hazard. Seen inside the depot on 3rd June 1968 are three local engines — BR Class 5 4-6-0 No 73133, LMS Class 5 4-6-0 No 45187 and an LMS Class 8F 2-8-0. (C. P. Stacey)

162)	The rising hills of the Peak District in the hazy background are covered with a sprinkling of winter snow at Chinley in January 1968, a favourite location for photographers in the dying days of steam. With steam leaking from its cylinders LMS Class 8F 2-8-0 No 48191, a 9F Heaton Mersey engine, passes a train of hoppers with a lengthy goods over one of the lofty stone viaducts associated with the area. (G. W. Sharpe)

163) It looks for all the world that the raised semaphore signal at the end of one of the platforms at Borough Bridge has released the troupe of enthusiasts from the same to enable them to gather round LMS Class 5 4-6-0 45305 which is being employed on the LCGB inspired 'Lancastrian' railtour on 6th April 1968. Despite the chalked shedcode of 8A Edge Hill (Liverpool), No 45305 is allocated to 8C Speke Junction. (N. E. Preedy)

164) LMS Class 8F 2-8-0 No 48504 stands in deep shadow outside its home base at 9K Bolton on 15th April 1968, next to an unidentified LMS Class 5 4-6-0. Prior to being allocated to Bolton in June 1966 No 48504 had spent a number of years in the West Midlands operating from Aston and Nuneaton sheds. Withdrawn in June 1968 from Bolton it was reduced to scrap three months later at Drapers, Hull. (R. Picton)

165)   In terms of a public relations exercise the final day of steam working on British Railways metals was a disgrace, as if the authorities couldn't wait to be rid of steam, instead of recognising its true value and giving it a good send-off. The 'fifteen guinea' special had no appropriate headboard and even the 'star' of the show BR *Britannia* Class 4-6-2 No 70013 *Oliver Cromwell,* seen near Horton on 11th August 1968 had stencilled 'nameplates'. (T. R. Amos)

166)   Dereliction in the sidings alongside 10D Lostock Hall shed on 6th April 1968. Cast to one side is an unwanted LMS Class 5 4-6-0 No 45421, with vandalised cab windows, two months after being condemned from Lostock Hall. Apart from serving at this shed No 45421 only worked at four other depots from 1957 onwards, these being at 8A Edge Hill (Liverpool), 12E Barrow, 12A Carlisle (Kingmoor) and 10C Fleetwood. (Mike Wood)

167) A smokescreen is laid over the countryside near to Droylsden (Manchester) as a duet of LMS Class 5 4-6-0's Nos 44874 and 45017, both allocated to 10A Carnforth but operating from 10D Lostock Hall, blast towards the camera at the head of a heavy enthusiasts special on 4th August 1968. Droylsden station, of joint London North Western/Lancashire & Yorkshire vintage closed during this same year. (T. R. Amos)

168) Another duet of locomotives, this time in the shape of two LMS Class 8F 2-8-0's, are partially hidden by stacks of coal adjacent to the brick built running shed at 10F Rose Grove on 6th April 1968. Unlike the previous 'live' picture, these locomotives, one of which is No 48310, their last fires have been long drawn, in the case of No 48310 in December 1967. All trace of Rose Grove shed today has long disappeared. (Mike Wood)

169) Yet another duo of steam engines captured by the camera. A resident LMS Class 5 4-6-0 No 45206 is in steam in the shed yard at 9D Newton Heath on 5th May 1968 in company with sister locomotive No 45025, a visitor from 10A Carnforth. After the closure of Newton Heath shed to steam on 1st July 1968, No 45206 became a stablemate of No 45025 at Carnforth. Both engines remained in service until the end of steam came along. (N. E. Preedy)

170) An enthusiast, complete with a brief case rather than a 'duffle-bag', sits on his haunches next to an LMS Class 5 4-6-0 in the shed yard at 10A Carforth on a July day in 1968. In front of him is the sole surviving BR Class 5 4-6-0 No 73069 underneath the coaling plant located at the southern end of the depot. At least Carnforth shed has survived the passage of time, albeit as a preservation centre. (G. W. Sharpe)

171)	Despite the mass introduction of overhead electrified wires over the years it is amazing, even today, how many former manual signalboxes are still in use on electrified sections of the London Midland Region. In May 1968 the manual box is still in action in the right of this picture, although the wires and point rodding are almost covered in weeds. LMS Class 5 4-6-0 No 45305 (8C Speke Junction) passes Edge Hill shed. (Christopher Fifield)

172)	A rain-soaked and miserable day at 10F Rose Grove in April 1968. In steam in front of the running shed are two LMS 'Black 5' 4-6-0's Nos 45382 and 45447, complete with numberplates, but minus shedplates, the code of 10F in stencilled lettering. To the right of these engines is an unidentified LMS Class 8F 2-8-0. Both Class 5's were condemned in June and August respectively. (C. P. Stacey)

173) A lengthy line-up of condemned locomotives await their inevitable fate on 'death row' at Swindon Works in September 1960. Three of the engines which can be identified are, from right to left — GWR 2251 Class 0-6-0 No 2264, formerly of 89C Machynlleth and withdrawn in September 1960 and two GWR 'Duke-Dogs' 4-4-0's Nos 9015 (89C Machynlleth - cond. June 1960) and 9004 (84J Croes Newydd - June 1960). (Ken Ellis)

174) Apart from the major railway works chopping up steam locomotives there were a host of outside contractors, both large and small, who did the same job. One of these contractors was Wards, a firm which had several different yards. Dumped at Beighton, Sheffield in March 1965 is LMS *Jubilee* Class 4-6-0 No 45672 *Anson,* late of 5A Crewe (North), having been withdrawn from there in November 1964. Behind *Anson* is a sister engine. (Stuart Pitchforth)

175) One of the major railway 'Graveyards' was at Darlington, a separate entity to the main workshop and many a fine engine came here to die. On 13th May 1962 all that is left of LNER L1 Class 2-6-4T No 67799 are the wheels, frames and coal bunker and no doubt these were soon to disappear. No 67799 had been taken out of service from 40E Colwick during this same month and the powers that be hadn't waited long to despatch the same to oblivion. (H.N. James)

176) A 'peep over the fence' at Cashmores, Great Bridge reveals a number of condemned engines on 16th April 1967. From left to right (with their last home depots in brackets) are — LMS Class 5 4-6-0 No 45091 (8F Springs Branch Wigan), LMS *Jubilee* Class 4-6-0 No 45627 *Sierra Leone* (8K Bank Hall), LMS Class 5 4-6-0's Nos 44935 (8B Warrington), 45329 (8C Speke Junction), GWR 5100 Class 2-6-2T No 4176 (2B Oxley) and BR Class 3 2-6-2T No 82009 (9H Patricroft). (T. R. Amos)

CHAPTER ELEVEN — PRESERVED LOCOMOTIVES

177) During 1987 steam made a welcome return to the Cambrian lines working out of Machynlleth. Locos from the Severn Valley were used and here we see a GWR *Manor* Class 4-6-0 back on its old stamping ground. No 7819 *Hinton Manor* is serviced at Barmouth before the return trip to Machynlleth on 31st May 1987. (N. E. Preedy)

178) LNER K4 Class 2-6-0 No 3442 (61994) *The Great Marquess* pauses at Sheffield station with a return British Rail test load working to Derby, shortly after restoration to main line running at the hands of the skilled staff at Bridgnorth, on the Severn Valley, seen on 30th June 1989. (J. D. Gomersall)

179) Former Somerset & Dorset Class 7F 2-8-0 No 53809, withdrawn from normal BR service from 82F Bath Green Park in June 1964, passes Gloucester yard on 16th September 1987, en route from Butterley to Salisbury to take part in rail tours. No 53809, in pristine condition, sports the old 'Pines Express' headboard. (N. E. Preedy)